THE COTTAGE GARDEN

Twigs Way

SHIRE PUBLICATIONS

Published in Great Britain in 2011 by Shire Publications Ltd, Midland House, West Way, Botley, Oxford OX2 0PH, United Kingdom.

44-02 23rd Street, Suite 219, Long Island City, NY 11101, USA.

E-mail: shire@shirebooks.co.uk   www.shirebooks.co.uk

A CIP catalogue record for this book is available from the British Library.

Shire Library no. 619.   ISBN-13: 978 0 74780 818 3

Twigs Way has asserted her right under the Copyright, Designs and Patents Act, 1988, to be identified as the author of this book.

Designed by Tony Truscott Designs, Sussex, UK and typeset in Perpetua and Gill Sans.
Printed in China through Worldprint Ltd.

11 12 13 14 15   10 9 8 7 6 5 4 3 2 1

COVER IMAGE
The artist Helen Allingham captured the cottage garden idyll for the newly urbanised population at the end of the nineteenth century.

TITLE PAGE IMAGE
Working in the garden was the country housewife's duty.

CONTENTS PAGE IMAGE
This postcard of 1915 epitomises the English cottage garden, gay with hollyhocks, scrambling roses and an old fruit tree.

ACKNOWLEDGEMENTS
Illustrations are acknowledged as follows:

Lyn Bascombe, page 13 (bottom); Bridgeman Art Library, page 40; Charles Cuthbert, page 10; British Library, cover image; English Heritage, page 34; Garden Museum, pages 14, 18 (both), 20 (all), 22, 24, 26 (top), 35 (top), 47 (bottom), 45, 49 (bottom), 50, 52 (top), 59 (all); iStockphoto, page 54 (top); Tony Jones, page 11 (bottom); publisher's collection, pages 4 and 29 (bottom); Amoret Tanner Collection, pages 6, 15, 16, 19 (both), 33 (top), 35 (bottom), 37, 38, 39 (bottom), 49 (top); Mark Werkmeister of East Lambrook Manor Garden, page 51; and Wikimedia, page 26 (bottom).

All other images are photographs taken by the author or are part of her collection.

Shire Publications is supporting the Woodland Trust, the UK's leading woodland conservation charity, by funding the dedication of trees.

CONTENTS

INTRODUCTION   4

PRODUCTIVE POVERTY   8

GROWING FOR SHOW AND BEAUTY   16

THE COTTAGE ORNÉE   24

VICTORIAN MORALITY AND IDEALISM   30

A BORDER OF ROMANTICS   40

RUS IN URBE   48

PLANTS FOR THE COTTAGE GARDEN   56

FURTHER READING   62

PLACES TO VISIT   63

INDEX   64

INTRODUCTION

HONEYSUCKLE at the gate, roses around the porch, tall spikes of lavender and marrows on the compost heap: everyone can envisage an 'English cottage garden'. But how exactly should it be defined? In the twenty-first century gardens of almost any size can be planted in 'cottage-garden' style, and even urban courtyards overflow with cottage-garden flowers. No longer confined to the country, the cottage or the poor cottager, it has become a design style. In the past, however, things were very different. For garden writers of the sixteenth and seventeenth centuries, the cottage garden was the province of the poor and industrious, providing food and physic through the year: a garden of utility, with beauty as incidental. For the poorer gentry of the eighteenth century it represented a rural idyll, a living nosegay of flowers to cover the shame of indigence; but by the nineteenth century morality had crept in by the garden gate and a well-tended plot was the sign of the God-fearing labourer.

Asked to define the cottage garden in 1893, the editor of *Cottage Gardening* stated:

> The term is one of which it is impossible to give a definition on hard and fast lines. It cannot be confined to one class of people, because many gentlemen and ladies live in cottages … we should say that a very good rule is that a cottage garden should be one all the labour in which is done by the occupier.

But the same periodical made it clear that gardens which contained annual bedding schemes would not be considered as true 'cottage gardens', however rural and humble the dwelling to which they were attached. Cottage gardens, it insisted, should overflow with jasmines, old roses, mignonette and hardy flowers. Walks should wind their way through plots so packed with blooms that even the walls of privies and pig-sties were to be covered in woodbine. In the eyes of the editor of *Cottage Gardening*, it was the very absence of a 'pretentious plan' that lent the charm to the

Opposite:
The garden at Anne Hathaway's Cottage, Warwickshire, has long been regarded as the epitome of the English cottage garden.

cottage garden, leaving the 'flowers to tell their own tale'. How paradoxical, then, that the second half of the twentieth century should see an outpouring of books instructing gardeners and designers how to plan their own 'cottage garden'.

For the purposes of this book, the cottage garden has been taken to be what the contemporaries of each of the periods covered might have

This Edwardian garden appears to owe more to the Arts and Crafts Movement than to the need to provide produce for the family.

Where the marjoram once, and sage and rue,
And balm and mint, with curled-leaf parsley grew,
And double marigolds and silver thyme,
And pumpkins 'neath the window used to climb;
And where I often, when a child, for hours
Tried through the pales to get the tempting flowers;
As lady's-laces, everlasting peas,
True-love-lies-bleeding, with the hearts at ease,
And golden-rods and tansy running high,
That o'er the pale-top smiled on passer-by'.

John Clare (1793–1864), 'The Cross Roads'

understood it to be. On the whole, they would agree that it should be relatively humble, relatively rural and relatively small, making up for its deficiencies of scale with rich, overflowing floral abundance.

Roses of all forms are an essential of the cottage garden, but none more so than the traditional ramblers and climbers. This hybrid briar rose illustrated the 1893 edition of *Cottage Gardening*.

PRODUCTIVE POVERTY

O UR WORD 'cottage' comes from the Middle English *cottar*, a peasant or farm labourer who, in return for work on the land, was allowed a small house and, if he was lucky, a small piece of land adjoining it. We have no illustrations or descriptions of the gardens attached to these humble dwellings but archaeology has given us a glimpse of the size and layout of these early cottage gardens. At the deserted medieval settlement of Wharram Percy, North Yorkshire, houses had 'crofts' of land of up to two-thirds of an acre associated with them. As well as his garden produce, a peasant with an area this size might have a small orchard, graze a pig or a cow, and produce useful coppiced hazel or willow in the boundary hedging. Boundary hedges were vital in a community where chickens, geese, ducks, pigs and even a calf might stray through the village; as the old saying goes, 'good fences make good neighbours'. In Chaucer's fourteenth-century *Nun's Priest's Tale*, a fence and ditch surround the widow's small back garden:

> A yerd she hadde, enclosed al aboute
> With stikkes, and a dry ditch with-oute.

Chaucer's widow grew coleworts, a type of loose-headed cabbage that was so important in the early medieval diet that it gave rise to the general use of the term *wort-gart* for a vegetable plot, replacing the Saxon term *laek tun*, or leek garden.

Evidence from monastic gardens from the twelfth to fifteenth centuries indicates that other popular vegetables of this period were onions, shallots, lettuce, leeks, leaf beet, skirrets, rampions, alexanders and carrots, and we can envisage these also filling the secular gardens of the villagers. Herbs were widely grown and used as medicines, as well as for flavouring foods. Rue, parsley, fennel, lovage, mint, chervil, borage, marigold and mallow were the most common, although wild herbs such as comfrey and wild thyme were also used. Fennel, mint, mugwort and wormwood might also be grown and brought into the house to rid it of smells and insects. Plants we think of as

Opposite:
Pot Marigolds, favourites of the cottage garden, were named in honour of the Virgin Mary.

weeds would have been eagerly sought out for salads or the pot, including chickweed, sowthistle and fat hen (*Chenopodium album*), taking pressure off the small garden space. Tithe lists for villages overseen by St Augustine's Abbey in Kent make it clear that the gardens there also contained doves, hens, geese, pigs and bees, as well as vegetables, vetches, hemp, apples and pears, all of which were duly recorded by the church tax inspectors.

A prosperous villager might have several fruit trees in his garden – pears, apples, quinces, damsons and medlars all being popular. Pears especially were long associated with the cottage garden, and by the thirteenth century a gardener might have either a Wardon or St Regula pear, both named after monasteries where these varieties had been developed.

Several cottagers' gardens have been created at the Weald and Downland Open Air Museum in West Sussex. The small fenced area around the thirteenth-century cottage known as 'Hangleton' contains cut-and-come-again plants, including green onions, hyssop, sage, parsley, leeks (cut like chives), and of course coleworts. To overcome the infertile, flinty chalk soil of the South Downs, the plants are placed in raised beds enriched with

The 'original' country cottage garden, a mix of herbs and vegetables, recreated for the 'Bayleaf' farmhouse at the Weald and Downland Open Air Museum in West Sussex.

Hurdle fencing, such as this at 'Poplar Cottage', Weald and Downland Open Air Museum, was essential for keeping wandering livestock and rabbits out of gardens.

A 'Tudor maid' picks lavender at the Weald and Downland Open Air Museum.

rubbish and manure, as they would have been in the Middle Ages. 'Bayleaf', a more prosperous yeoman's homestead of *c*.1500, has more land associated with it than 'Hangleton', and within the sturdy hedging there is an orchard and an area of coppice, as well as a large kitchen garden and a separate herb garden. Coleworts, peas, leeks, parsley and beans still predominate but there is also room for sweet herbs such as lavender and marjoram.

During the Elizabethan period a law stipulated that all newly built cottages should have access to 4 acres of land, more than enough for an orchard, pasture and garden. Like many laws, this one was honoured more in the breaking than the keeping, and the cottager's plot remained on the whole a small one.

The first book to include instruction on what should be in the cottager and yeoman's garden was published in 1573. Thomas Tusser's *Five Hundred Pointes of Good Husbandrie* was full of advice for yeomen, farmers and their wives. The garden was the wife's responsibility, and Tusser tells her what she should be doing each month:

In March and in April, from morning to night,
In sowing and setting good housewives delight;
To have in a garden or other like plot,
To trim up their house, and to furnish their pot.

In September the good housewife should collect wild strawberries in the woods to plant in her garden, and the vision that Tusser gives is not far removed from the nineteenth-century cottage garden, with 'Gooseberry, Respis [raspberry] and Roses, all three … With strawberries under them trimly agree'. Elsewhere in the garden, Tusser expected there to be daffodils, primroses, columbines, rosemary, gillyflowers, hollyhocks and carnations, as well as herbs for strewing (on the floor of the house), and for cooking. Gillyflowers were originally any plant that flowered in July, but the word came to mean pinks, sweet rocket and wallflowers especially, all stalwarts of the cottage garden. In the vegetable plot, Tusser recommends 'perseneps, cabbegis, turneps, carrets' and beans, as well as 'runcivall peas'. Runcivall, or Rouncival, peas were a large type of pea that had been developed in the fifteenth century in the hospital gardens of St Mary of Roncesvalles at Charing Cross, London. They became instantly popular. In addition to looking pretty, all of the flowers in this Elizabethan cottage garden would have had a use. Until the nineteenth century herbs used by the housewife to treat coughs and colds, wounds, sprains and even broken limbs. Many cottage-garden plants have common names that reveal what they could be used for, such as woundwort (*Stachys officinalis*), knitbone or comfrey (*Symphytum officinale*) and lungwort (*Pulmonaria officinalis*).

Hollyhocks have long been favourites in the cottage garden. Brought back from the Holy Land by pilgrims or crusaders, they are from the same botanical family as Britain's native mallow, or hock, to which they have many similarities – hence the name 'holy-hock'.

An old cottage with its proud mix of traditional flowers and herbs.

For the cottage housewife who did not appreciate her garden advice in couplets, relief came in the form of *The Country House-wives' Garden*, published by William Lawson in 1618. Topics covered by Lawson included the layout of

Right: Wild violets are one of the native British plants grown in cottage gardens. This illustration is from the Reverend C. A. Johns's *Flowers of the Field* (first published in 1853), Gertrude Jekyll's favourite book as a child.

Below right: William Lawson's *Country House-wives' Garden* contains lists of the flowers and herbs that he expected his readers to plant in their gardens.

Below: A lavender plant depicted in a seventeenth-century herbal. Lavender was used in cooking, drinks, and as a soothing medicine.

VIOLA CANINA, *and* V. ODORATA.

3 *Lavendula minor, five Spica.*
La uander Spike.

THE
COUNTRY HOUSE-WIVES
GARDEN,

Containing rules for Herbs, and Seeds, of common use, with their times and feasons when to fet and fow them.

Together

With the Husbandry of Bees, publi-
fhed with fecrets very neceffary for every Houf-
wife: As alfo divers new Knots for Gardens.

The Contents fee at large, in the laft Page.

Genef. 2. 29.
*I have given unto you every Herbe, and every Tree, that fhall be to you
for meat.*

LONDON,
Printed by *William Wilfon,* for *George
Sawbridge,* at the Bible on Ludgate-hill,
neer Fleet-bridge, 1660.

the garden, herbs and plants to be included, general rules for gardening and beekeeping. However small the area available, Lawson recommends that the garden be divided into two parts, a kitchen garden, and a flower or 'summer' garden. Lawson reasoned that if onions and parsnips were to be planted in the flower garden the flowers would 'suffer some disgrace'. Some herbs might be grown in both gardens, with violets, borage, roses and lavender being used to edge the vegetable plot. So successful were these instruction books for country gardens that by 1683 John Worlidge in his *Systema Horticultura* (second edition) was able to state confidently that 'there is scarce a Cottage in most of the Southern Parts of England but hath a proportionable Garden, so great a delight do most men take in it'.

Keeping bees was often the responsibility of the housewife rather than the husband. William Lawson included instructions on beekeeping in his *Country House-wives' Garden* of 1618.

Daniels'
Unrivalled
Florists'
Flowers

GROWING FOR SHOW AND BEAUTY

'FLORISTS' FLOWERS', so called from the flower collectors, or 'florists', who devoted their leisure hours to them, were the original subjects of horticultural competition. In the seventeenth and early eighteenth centuries these contests concentrated on what were then expensive bulbs and flowers such as tulips, ranunculus and auriculas, well beyond the purse of the cottager of that period, but by the later eighteenth century the varieties of flowers admitted to florists' societies had widened considerably and prices had dropped. The working classes enthusiastically embraced the new opportunities. In 1897 Beeton's *All about Gardening* (new edition) listed the following as florists' flowers suitable for show: dahlia, hollyhock, chrysanthemum, tulip, polyanthus, auricula, heartsease or pansy, ranunculus, anemone, carnation, pink, picotee and hyacinth, all easily grown in the cottage garden.

Soon 'growing for show' became a common feature of the cottage plot, despite the minimal value of even the first prize. Set aside from the overflowing borders, plants being grown for competition would be given a special area, often with some form of canvas shelter, against a wall, or with a rudimentary cold frame for protection or forcing. In 1847 *The Horticultural Magazine* recorded that 'There are many small gardens, even now, in the Mile End Road, with their canvas houses looking, in the season, like an encampment.' By the late nineteenth century small glasshouses and glazed lean-tos became a frequent sight in cottage gardens, where half-hardy flowers would be overwintered, cosseted by those eager to beat their rivals. Where gardens were too small to accommodate them, glasshouses even made an appearance on allotments.

Large regional and national societies devoted specific shows to the various flowers at appropriate times of year: tulips and anemones in May, carnations and picotees in August, chrysanthemums in September. Smaller regional shows might combine these with fruit or vegetables: strawberries in June along with the pinks and picotees, melons and gooseberries in August. Village societies often restricted themselves to just one large show a year,

Opposite:
By the late nineteenth century the definition of the florists' flower had widened, including, here, calceolaria, pink and white picotee, and penstemon.

Auriculas were one of the original florists' flowers and became a popular show flower for the cottager.

This patch of the country garden come to town has the essentials of a rose arch and a mix of flowers and vegetables, as well as a little glasshouse for raising tender and show plants.

possibly with a smaller one in spring. Shows also differed according to the region of the country. In the 1890s Lancashire men, for example, were known for concentrating their efforts on gooseberries, auriculas, pinks and carnations.

Although national shows were the privilege of the gentry, regional shows had separate 'cottager' classes for those ambitious enough to travel to them. But it was the village horticultural shows that were the real home of the cottage gardener. The highlight of the

COTTAGE GARDEN SHOW

(In Connection with the Parishes of Holy Trinity, Christ Church, and All Souls),

WILL BE HELD

ON MONDAY, AUG. 4TH, 1884,

IN

CHRIST CHURCH SCHOOLS.

Prizes will be offered in the following Classes of Exhibits :—

CLASS I.

Flowering Plants in Pots and Boxes.

1, Roses ; 2, Scented Geraniums ; 3, Ivy Geraniums ; 4, Geraniums of other sorts ; 5, Fuschias ; 6, Musks ; 7, Ice Plants ; 8, Begonias ; 9, Coleus ; 10, Calceolarias ; 11, Lobelias ; 12, Cactus.

CLASS II.

A.—Cut Flowers (*Six blooms in each variety*).

13, Roses ; 14, Geraniums ; 15, Fuschias ; 16, Carnations and Picotees ; 17, Dahlias ; 18, Sunflowers ; 19, Hollyhocks ; 20, Bouquets.

B.—Wild Flowers

21, Bouquets of Wild Flowers and Grasses ; 22, Ferns and Mosses.

CLASS III.

23, Ferns ; 24, Acacias ; 25, Myrtles ; 26, other Evergreen Shrubs.

CLASS IV.

27, Kidney Potatoes (12) ; 28, Round Potatoes (12) ; 29, Cauliflowers (2) ; 30, Onions (8) ; 31, Cabbages (2) ; 32, Vegetable Marrows (2 fit for table) ; 33, Tomatoes (6) ; 34, Turnips (6) ; 35, Cucumbers (2) ; 36, Carrots (6) ; 37, Peas (6 pods) ; 38, Beans (6 pods of any kind) ; 39, Collection of Vegetables, (six kinds).

CLASS V.—Birds.

40, Clear Yellow or Buff Norwich Canaries ; 41, Marked Yellow or Buff Norwich Canaries ; 42, Crested Norwich Canaries ; 43, Any other variety of Canary ; 44, Gold Finch Mules ; 45, Any other variety of Mules ; 46, Pigeons ; 47, Parrots.

CLASS VI.—Domestic Animals.

48, Rabbits.

CLASS VII.—Industrial Exhibits.

49, Models ; 50, Useful Articles ; 51, Ornamental Articles.

CLASS VIII.

52, Honey-in-Comb.

Local shows typically took place in August, to allow time for most vegetables to crop, although a smaller spring show might be held for spring flowers and early crops. At this show there are also classes for livestock.

village year, these incorporated flowers, vegetables and produce – plates of radishes alongside pots of home-made jam and lacework. Such competitions were considered a healthy pursuit for the labouring classes. Gardening periodicals carried letters and editorials giving examples not only of individuals but of whole villages saved from moral decline by the simple expedient of a local horticultural society and its shows. Horticultural societies often included the words 'mutual improvement' in their titles, and the shows emphasised the ideal of striving for betterment.

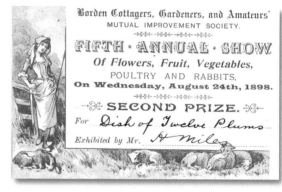

Borden Cottagers, Gardeners, and Amateurs'
MUTUAL IMPROVEMENT SOCIETY.

FIFTH · ANNUAL · SHOW

Of Flowers, Fruit, Vegetables,
POULTRY AND RABBITS,
On Wednesday, August 24th, 1898.

SECOND PRIZE.

For *Dish of Twelve Plums*

Exhibited by Mr. H. Miles

The Borden Show included poultry and rabbits as well as the usual flowers and vegetables.

Prizes at cottage-garden shows sometimes took the form of seeds, and a writer in the February 1893 issue of *Cottage Gardening* recommended that seeds of better or improved varieties should be given, so that cottagers would not devote their time and effort to inferior sorts – although presumably the winners of the prizes were the ones who least needed this extra help. Seed distribution was sometimes seen as a starting point for the formation of a local horticultural or cottage-garden society, providing the initial spark of interest. The editor of *Cottage Gardening* claimed that:

This early example of a cottage garden society prize ticket is highly decorated. The members are obviously expected to use the Latin names for their plants.

A much-prized medal for 'a collection of vegetables' at the Morden Cottage Garden Society show in 1907.

Seedsmen such as Carters created improved and tested strains from the late nineteenth century onwards, and, although these were sometimes beyond the pocket of the Victorian cottager, seeds and plants might be given as prizes at horticultural shows.

The distribution of seeds is a proper and indeed necessary step in the case of those who are interested in the subject of cottage garden societies, and the more isolated the locality the greater the want of some such help, for cottagers have few opportunities and less means of securing improved varieties of vegetables.

The small scale of many of these shows led to confusion in the naming of the varieties that were shown. Pinks, for example, one of the easiest to grow and most popular cottage florist flowers, had thousands of varieties. In 1834 Thomas Hogg of Paddington Green listed such delights as 'Berkshire Buffalo', 'Beauty of Ugliness', 'Cheese's Miss Cheese' and 'Hopkin's Scarecrow'. One of the most popular and sweetest-smelling pinks, 'Mrs Sinkins', was originally bred from seed raised in the Slough workhouse garden by the master of the workhouse, Mr Sinkins. It had come a long way by the time it graced rural cottage gardens. Despite obvious difficulties in showing, the hollyhock also became a show flower, along with pansies, tulips, chrysanthemums and dahlias. Vegetables and fruits appealed to those who had little time for anything unproductive, and marrows, radishes, runner beans and leeks joined the show catalogues. Growing six matching beans or the longest, straightest carrots kept many a man from the alehouse.

In some areas gooseberries had specific societies and shows. They had always had a special place in the cottage garden. Easily grown, they were a favourite fruit for cooking and preserving. As late as the 1940s, they were

Prize marrows have long been stalwarts of the village horticultural show.

recommended as a favourite with Bird's custard, falling out of favour only when year-round imported fruits became available. In 1896 a 'Gentleman of Great Practical Experience' recommended that an average cottage gardener should plant as many as a dozen bushes, more if he had children, but the gooseberry could promise more than mere culinary delights. Fame, if not fortune, awaited the member of a gooseberry society who could grow a

Supplement to *Amateur Gardening*, January 16th. 1926.

960

SEVEN GOOD GOOSEBERRIES.

Top Left-hand Variety—" TELEGRAPH."   Top Right-hand Variety—" LEVELLER."
Pale Variety—" CARELESS.
Small Red Variety—" IRONMONGER."   Large Red Variety—" WHINHAM'S INDUSTRY."
Lower Left-hand Variety—" CRITERION."   Lower Right-hand Variety—" LEADER."
[*Natural Order, Saxifrageae. Sax frage Family.*]

Drawing prepared for Amateur Gardening. [*Copyright.*]   *Co-Inqriders. Colour Printers. London*

Gooseberries were once widely grown in red, yellow, green and 'white'. In the late nineteenth century varieties included 'Lancashire Lad', 'Yellow Champagne', 'Gregory's Perfection', 'White Honey' and 'Beaumont's Red'.

22

gooseberry larger than those of his fellows. The first gooseberry societies were formed by the hand-loom weavers of Cheshire, Lancashire, Yorkshire and parts of the Midlands in the mid-eighteenth century. By 1786 an annual gooseberry register was printed, listing all the gooseberry shows and the weights of winning fruits, recorded in pennyweights (dwt) and grains. The register demonstrates the extraordinary dedication of the societies' members to developing giant gooseberries. From a humble 10 dwt (15.5 grams) in 1786, winning weights increased to 32 dwt in 1825, and a staggering 37 dwt 7 grains for a record-breaking berry in the 1850s. Gooseberry shows were an essential part of the societies' activities, with 171 shows listed in the 1845 register. As befitted the humble origins of the gooseberry clubs, shows were held mainly in pubs or licensed clubs, with some show regulations stipulating how much drink was to be purchased during the show. Charles Darwin is said to have used the records of the Gooseberry Register as evidence for the mutability of species, and he himself cultivated fifty-four varieties, although he did not show them.

what does your garden grow?

GOOSEBERRIES!

.. *serve them with*

BIRD'S
CUSTARD
and use less sugar

EAT more fruit and eat it with Bird's Custard. That is the way to save on sugar, and that is the way to add nourishment to meals. For BIRD'S CUSTARD is easily digested GOODNESS. And, of course, there's the famous extra-special flavour of BIRD'S CUSTARD to persuade children to take their daily quota of milk.

BIRD'S CUSTARD AND JELLIES

Gooseberries are good enough for a king, but they are so easily grown that their real value is not appreciated, and because they are common they are overlooked. However, let no cottage gardener despise them, but plant a dozen bushes at least; two dozen will not be too many for the average household.

Cottage Gardening: A Practical Manual (1896)

Gooseberries were the traditional dessert fruit until displaced by imported fruits in the late twentieth century. This wartime advertisement stresses their vitamin content.

THE COTTAGE ORNÉE

THE ROMANTIC MOVEMENT of the late eighteenth century enticed a steady stream of social misfits, intellectuals and artists to retreat to cottages in the country. They were followed by the fashionable and the financially challenged, some playing at being cottage dwellers, others taking it up as a reality. These intellectual escapees gathered wild flowers to plant in their gardens and left honeysuckle and hops to climb unhindered over the rustic bower. The cottage *ornée* was born.

Refugees from society were the first to invade the rural idyll, probably much to the confusion of its labouring inhabitants. Sarah Ponsonby and Eleanor Butler were fleeing both their parents and social norms when they settled together at Plas Newydd, Llangollen, in 1780. Here they intended to live the good life, raising their own hens and cows, growing their own food and gardening. Plas Newydd was larger than the average cottage, with five rooms set in 4 acres of land, which was just as well, as the Ladies of Llangollen, as they became known, spent what time they had over from their gardening pursuits entertaining the hordes of writers, artists and aesthetes who descended on them. Not originally intellectuals themselves, Eleanor and Sarah now devoted themselves to reading, learning languages and beautifying the gardens in the latest picturesque style. Their favourite book was Rousseau's *Julie: ou la nouvelle Heloïse*, with its evocative descriptions of the heroine's 'wild' garden full of birds and flowers. Plas Newydd, with its model dairy, Gothic bird-table, shrubberies and artfully tumbling brook, may seem to us beyond the scope of a 'cottage garden', but its visitors always thought of it as one. Its carefully contrived mix of wild flowers and cultivated ones, traditional and new, charmed visitors with its cottage-garden style. Roses, lilacs, syringas, pinks, primroses and violets jostled with brightly coloured dahlias and florist flowers. The Ladies did employ a gardener but did much of the work themselves, thus coming under the definition of cottage gardeners offered by the editor of *Cottage Gardening*.

Among the visitors to Plas Newydd were the Wordsworths, themselves in the vanguard of intellectual cottage dwellers. Fresh from the rigours of

Opposite:
This delightful cottage *ornée* with its colourful garden would have been the envy of eighteenth-century romantic intellectuals.

The delights of gardening lured many a Regency lady towards the supposed idyll of the countryside.

When the Wordsworths left Dove Cottage for the more substantial Rydal Mount, they recorded their feelings in a poem about their orchard garden. They were much distressed to hear of the changes made later by their writer friend Thomas de Quincey.

Cambridge, William Wordsworth was touring the Lake District when he saw what was to become his home, Dove Cottage, in the village of Grasmere. Despite frequent visitors, including Samuel Taylor Coleridge, Thomas de Quincey and Walter Scott, the Wordsworths devoted much of their time to the small orchard and garden. The small gardens were steeply terraced into the side of the hill, and the Wordsworths filled them with native and wild flowers, including wild thyme and orchids brought from the lakeside. In her journal, Dorothy Wordsworth carefully noted the flowers as they changed with the seasons, from snowdrops and hepaticas, primroses and celandines, through to foxgloves and roses. The orchard bore apples, plums and pears, and a bower allowed them to sit among the bees and birds while writing their poetry. Dorothy and William did much of the work themselves, planting the slips and seeds they had obtained from the local vicar and the neighbouring farmers' wives, although, unlike truly poor cottagers, they also bought shrubs from the local nurseryman.

DOVE COTTAGE, FROM THE GARDEN.
"Thou little nook of mountain ground.
Sweet garden-orchard eminently fair.
The loveliest spot that man hath ever found."
Farewell to Dove Cottage.

> Sweet Garden-orchard! of all spots that are
> The loveliest surely man hath ever found.
> Farewell! we leave thee to heaven's peaceful care.
> Thee and the cottage which thou dost surround...
>
> Dear Spot! whom we have watched with tender heed,
> Bringing thee chosen plants and blossoms blown
> Among the distant mountains, flower and weed
> Which thou hast taken to thee as thy own...
>
> William Wordsworth (1770–1850), 'Dove Cottage Garden'

Rather more practically, if less successfully, Fanny Burney and her refugee French husband, Alexandre d'Arblay, took up cottage living, at Great Bookham in Surrey, for the first time in 1793. Alexandre was a former artillery officer and his grasp of vegetable cultivation left much to be desired at a time when the d'Arblays, like most cottagers, were dependent on what they could grow. In a letter to her father, Fanny wrote:

> Seeds are sowing where plants ought to be reaping, and plants are running to seed while they are thought not yet at maturity. Our garden, therefore, is not the most profitable thing in the world; but Mr d'A. assures me it is to be the staff of our table and existence.

Cabbages were the only produce they had yet had, and even these had been running to seed before the d'Arblays noticed they were ready for the plate. The garden was not all vegetables, for Fanny went on to describe the extraordinary efforts her husband was making in moving all the flowering shrubs and roses from one part of the garden to another, 'till they have all danced round as far as the space allow...'. Fortunately the

Olney Vicarage, Buckinghamshire, home of the poet William Cowper (1731–1800). His letters described the gardens and the three hares that he tamed and which played in the house and garden.

OLNEY VICARAGE.

27

Fanny Burney must have been dismayed looking at the empty plot outside her cottage, just as this mother is doing.

COTTAGE GARDENERS.

family was saved from starvation by the success of Fanny Burney's novel *Camilla*, the proceeds of which were used to build another house, which they named Camilla Cottage, and their gardening trials recommenced.

So fashionable was cottage living among the leisured classes in the Regency period that it attracted the witty attentions of Jane Austen. In *Sense and Sensibility*, the foppish Robert Ferrars informs Marianne Dashwood that:

> I am excessively fond of a cottage; there is always so much comfort, so much elegance about them. And I protest, if I had any money to spare, I should buy a little land and build one myself … I advise every body who is going to build, to build a cottage. My friend Lord Courtland came to me the other day on purpose to ask my advice, and laid before me three different plans of Bonomi's [an architect of the Greek style]. I was to decide on the best of them. 'My dear Courtland,' said I, immediately throwing them all into the fire, 'do not adopt either of them, but by all means build a cottage.'

Unfortunately Jane Austen does not go on to tell us what type of garden Robert Ferrars would have his friends create around their palatial cottages. Austen's own family homes, the rectories at Steventon and Chawton in Hampshire, were cultivated by her family – Mrs Austen donning a gardening smock for the task of digging up potatoes. The Austen family grew syringas, honeysuckle, hollyhocks and Sweet Williams, an established shrubbery walk in the latest fashion of the early nineteenth century. Flowers and vegetables mixed in a cottage garden with more social abandon than Mr Ferrars might have thought appropriate.

In 1759 the naturalist and clergyman Gilbert White of Selborne, Hampshire, recorded that his flower gardens contained 'planted [in the new bank] flowers in two rows: the upper row was columbines, French honeysuckles & rose campions, at a yard apart, the lower row all Sweet Williams at a foot apart...' The gardens were full of scent, with Persian jasmine (lilac), sweet peas, roses and wallflowers, and bright with the colour of sunflowers, marvel of Peru and amaranthus. White also grew all his own vegetables and fruits, including cucumbers 13 inches in length, cropped by the hundred – almost unheard of in an amateur's garden. Home-grown cantaloup melons also enriched his dining table forty times in one year.

The Austen family inhabited that class of 'cottage' classed as 'genteel' and we might look to more low-born authors such as Thomas Hardy and the pastoral poet John Clare for true reliance on a cottage garden. Thomas Hardy was born in 1840 in a typical Dorset cob-and-thatch cottage built by his great-grandfather. Now owned by the National Trust, it is surrounded by gardens and orchard in the style that Hardy would have known in his childhood, and which he recorded in books such as *Under the Greenwood Tree*. Potatoes, cabbages, dahlias, fuchsias and bees fill the gardens in Hardy's novel.

With its vine over the door, fashionable ferns and the well-dressed woman, this is a rather up-market Victorian cottage garden.

Thomas Hardy's Birthplace, Bockhampton

Thomas Hardy's childhood home in Dorset influenced his novels on country life. The cottage, built by his great-grandfather, is now owned by the National Trust.

29

VICTORIAN MORALITY AND IDEALISM

POVERTY, idleness and drunkenness were, according to contemporary social commentators, the downfall of the labouring classes in the nineteenth century, and where better to address those concerns than in the garden. Gardening was, as Samuel Reynolds Hole (1819–1904), Dean of Rochester, declared, both a 'pleasant and a profitable occupation of leisure hours', although he had more leisure hours than most of his parishioners. He continued:

> He who persuades a man to garden [will have] transformed a drone into a bee, and … done more to keep his brother from drunkenness than all the pamphlets that were ever printed … He will have added not only to our respectability but to our food supply.

Dean Hole was eloquent in the support not only of cottage gardens but of allotments too (themselves often confusingly called 'cottage gardens'), appealing to landowners and county councils to provide allotment land, 'from our love as Christians and from our duty as patriots'. He lived for forty-three years in the village of Caunton, Nottinghamshire, before becoming Dean and was famous as a rose-grower and the founder of the National Rose Show.

The Dean was not alone in his belief that a garden overflowing with produce was the key to society's salvation. A Mr Middlemiss, head gardener to A. Pott of Tunbridge Wells, wrote to the periodical *The Cottage Gardener* detailing how the establishment of a small village horticultural society had transformed the villagers of Etal, Northumberland. Before the foundation of the society the villagers had apparently been belligerents, whose principal entertainment had been swearing, drinking and cock-fighting. Within a year of the society's formation, Mr Middlemiss recounted that:

> Pieces of ground which then bore nothing but crops of nettles and thistles are now clothed with the gayest beauties of the floral kingdom, or groaning under the loads of the finest vegetables that can possibly be grown. It is astonishing that in such a short space of time such a revolution could take

Opposite:
The sweet honeysuckle twining around the old fruit tree was evoked as an ideal image of Victorian working-class marriage by sentimental writers such as 'Rosa' in *The Cottage Gardener*.

31

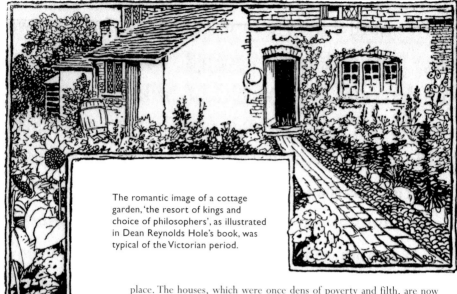

The romantic image of a cottage garden, 'the resort of kings and choice of philosophers', as illustrated in Dean Reynolds Hole's book, was typical of the Victorian period.

place. The houses, which were once dens of poverty and filth, are now changed into neat white-washed cottages.

Cottage-garden and horticultural societies regularly included regulations insisting that members were morally upright and sober, and some held writing and reading competitions, taking their educational remit well beyond simple planting and sowing. Gardeners from the local 'big house' would be well positioned to help other members of a society, as trainee gardeners were recommended to study hard, including subjects as diverse as Latin, geology, geometry and, of course, botany. Magazines for 'florists' were also firmly convinced of the moral benefit of their subscribers' interest. *The Horticultural Magazine* warned that 'unless something be done to provide the mechanic with means of indulging in the practice of Floriculture, he will have recourse to the public-house and skittle-ground for less healthy amusements'.

Prizegivings at the annual shows were usually accompanied by an address by the local landowner or vicar. At the annual meeting of the Halesworth (Suffolk) Allotment Gardeners Association, plotholders

assembled in the school room with banners proclaiming 'Give the first fruits of your allotment to the Lord' … After which Mr Johnstone addressed some useful remarks to his tenants, first on their moral and religious conduct, the education of their children etc, and then on the management of their ground.

In 1839 the nurseryman Thomas Hogg declared that 'horticulture is a pursuit at once rational and amusing; it gives health and recreation alike to the body and the mind'.

Even the flowers chosen for the cottage garden were given a moral overtone. According to the editor of *Cottage Gardening*, Michaelmas daisies were 'homely', and simple single flowers were preferable to 'fancy' double varieties. Showiness was to be avoided by both the cottage garden and the cottager. Steady perseverance and an adherence to utility were also the themes of Robert Adamson in the foreword to his 1856 book *The Cottage Garden*. He began:

> This Treatise being intended for the guidance of the cottager in the cultivation and general management of his garden, I have guarded against recommending anything inconsistent with such limited means as a cottager is supposed to possess, and which, when

Cottage Gardeners' Society Writing Competition

A labouring man, who had never learned to read, noticed that the clergyman put on spectacles when reading the service in church on Sunday.

He thought he should be able to read too if he got a pair of spectacles.

He put on a pair, and tried to read a newspaper.

Finding that he could not read with this pair, he asked for a better one.

The shopman showed him several pairs, but as the labourer was not satisfied with any of them the shopman said he was afraid the man could not read.

The labourer angrily replied, "Of course I can't. If I knew how to read, I should not require spectacles."

He left the shop disappointed and offended, but soon learnt that more is required to enable a man to read than a pair of spectacles.

Eliza Cook.

Cottage garden societies did not interest themselves only with their members' gardens; general social and moral improvement was also their concern, seen here in the form of a writing competition.

The morality of the cottage garden was lost on the designer who placed this garden around a 'pub' at the Chelsea Flower Show in 2005.

A garden full of vegetables indicated an upright and moral cottager to the Victorian mind. Frederick Ault recorded the labourers' cottages in Oxfordshire, including this one in the village of Shellingford.

combined with steady perseverance and economy, may cause even a small garden to produce a regular supply of useful fruits, vegetables and flowers.

Many a parsonage garden set a fine example to the village. In Bitton, Gloucestershire, the Reverend Henry Thomas Ellacombe and his son Henry Nicholson Ellacombe (later Canon) (1822–1916) created a glorious garden in an acre and a half. Canon Ellacombe defined the 'proverbial' parsonage garden as ' not large … with little glass and no pretention to a high class garden … a home for hundreds of good old-fashioned flowers' – in fact a garden in the country cottage style. He regarded 'a country parson without some knowledge of plants … as incomplete as a country parsonage without a garden'. Gardens

What magic power causes the lovely blossoms to bloom so profusely when crowded in the small corner of ground belonging to a workman's Cottage, the same flowers proving very ordinary under a trained Gardener's care? Love is the magic power … which the flowers repay a thousand fold.

M.R. Gloag, *A Book of English Gardens*, 1906.

were even a bridge between the parson and his flock, with plants and gardening advice flowing from the parsonage garden to the rest of the cottage garden plots. The vicar of Buckland Newton in Dorset, the Reverend James Venables (1770–1850), went even further in the practicalities of helping his flock to grow. In 1816 he wrote the first article on compost, entitled 'On enriching the Soil of Gardens by fresh vegetable Manure'. It made him famous, and he was awarded the Horticultural Society Medal that same year.

Morality also extended to the actual gardening, with women confined to the sweet-smelling flowers and men to the rather rougher vegetables. Flora Thompson, recalling her country childhood in *Lark Rise to Candleford*, records that the women tended the flowers and herbs in the garden while the menfolk went to the allotment. The same author gives us descriptions of the various gardens in the hamlets she lived in at the end of

Instruction abounded for the new cottage gardener. This example was written by Joseph Paxton, head gardener for the Duke of Devonshire at the rather grander gardens of Chatsworth.

'A marvel of quality and economy' sums up the needs of the vicarage or rectory garden following the general fall in clerical income in the nineteenth century.

Ryton Rectory.

Ryton Rectory, Northumberland. The rectory was a substantial building and had quite grand gardens. Canon Henry Nicholson Ellacombe decried the fashion for bedding plants in rectory gardens, holding that they should be the repositories of old-fashioned plants.

Opposite:
A delightful cottage garden on the Isle of Wight, from M. R. Gloag's *A Book of English Gardens*.

the nineteenth century. The garden of the postmistress at Candleford contained the necessary earth closet, wells, beehives and vegetables, but there was still room for flower borders 'crowded with jonquils, auriculas, forget-me-nots and other spring flowers ... rose bushes, and lavender and rosemary and a bush apple tree'. In the irregular square of a lower garden there were Michaelmas daisies, red-hot pokers and old-fashioned pompom dahlias in autumn, along with peonies and pinks. Other village gardens echoed each other as seeds and slips were passed from one garden to another. A similar garden provided a hiding place for Susan, the heroine of Alison Uttley's *The Country Child*, based on her own childhood in Victorian Derbyshire. Here the kitchen garden was crammed with currants and gooseberries – 'smooth yellow balloons, filled with wine' – while pinks, mignonette and musk grew among the vegetables.

Few moralists concerned themselves with the contents of the pig-sty, but for many cottagers the garden held more than just plants. Bees, pigs, rabbits, hens and ducks were all to be accommodated if the family was to have meat and eggs with their meals. In the Middle Ages pigs and chickens shared the yard and sometimes even the house, but by the Victorian period pigs were usually confined in a sty at the bottom of the garden. The author of *The Cottage Gardener* (published in 1856) stated that 'A portion of the garden ought to be allotted for ... a small tool house, washing house, pig-sty, privy and dung pit – it being impossible that any cottager and his family can be comfortable where any of the above requisites are unprovided'. A pig

> Every labourer should have apple-tree, plum-tree and cherry-tree, his bushes of gooseberries and currants, his potatoes and greens, in addition to his garden of flowers. He should refresh his mind with the ornamental, and his body with the useful.
>
> Dean Reynolds Hole, *In Our Gardens*, 1899

> Let the blooming creepers round our cottage porch instruct us, and lead us to twine our hopes and affections around 'those things that are above', around 'Him whose strength is made perfect in our weakness'.
>
> 'Rosa', *The Cottage Gardener*, August 1849

could provide manure that, mixed with the water from clothes and other washing, formed a rich liquid. Manure from the sty could be put straight onto the garden, along with slops and night soil from the privy.

Rabbits occupied a combination of roles as pet, pest and prospective meal. Despite strict game laws, most cottagers had access to wild rabbits, often from the poacher, but keeping domestic rabbits allowed a continuous supply, in return for scraps and some grain. In the words of *The Cottager's Companion* (1822), 'the fecundity of the rabbit is beyond expectation', and the creatures would reward the cottager well for the care taken. *Cottage Gardening* was more cautious, stating that 'Those who keep rabbits not simply as pets, but with a view to getting some little return, should get them as early as possible into a condition for killing' (December 1892). The editor, William Robinson, seems to have had a soft spot for pets, as his opinion on hens was that they should be killed off at two years old, but 'of course it makes a difference if [they] are houschold pets'. Other pets also crept into the cottage garden, and in 1893 *Cottage Gardening* was called upon for advice on how to hibernate tortoises and how to breed guinea pigs. Ducks and geese are frequently portrayed in paintings of cottage gardens, and the white Aylesbury

Pigs were ubiquitous in cottage gardens, providing ham for salting or drying, fat, bristles and a handy means of 'recycling' household waste.

duck and Toulouse goose were the most commonly kept birds, being excellent for meat and eggs. Khaki Campbells, the supreme egg-laying ducks, were introduced by Mrs Campbell in the late nineteenth century.

Bees were perhaps the most ubiquitous inhabitants of the cottage garden, providing honey in the centuries when sugar was a luxury of the upper classes, and performing pollination without which fruit trees would be bare. Bee skeps were simply made of coiled straw and perched on small stands, sometimes with a small shelter from rain and wind, or just a piece of old sacking and an upturned pot.

Although it may look unstable, the provision of a stand and shelter was a luxury for bees in a cottage garden. This one was illustrated in *Cottage Gardening*, 21 December 1892.

Pest, pet or pot? The rabbit has always played a difficult role in the cottage garden.

A BORDER OF ROMANTICS

TIMELESS VISIONS of the cottage garden came under threat in the late nineteenth century as the shadow of urbanisation crept outwards. In 1879 Francis Horner observed that the old gardens of the handloom weavers that once lay on the edges of towns were now 'deeply bedded' in suburbia, their gardens swallowed up by bricks and mortar. Further out in the countryside, the urban fashion for gaudy bedding designs threatened the traditional cottage flowers, and the use of patented medicines resulted in the neglect of herb patches. The unexpected saviours of the cottage garden were artists, writers and garden designers, many closely linked with the Arts and Crafts Movement, prizing heritage and tradition above novelty and invention.

William Morris (1834–96), leader of the Arts and Crafts Movement, incorporated cottage-garden plants and flowers into his textiles and wallpaper designs: honeysuckle, jasmine, sunflower, rose, acanthus and vine all twine and twirl and lift their heads in his tapestries and fabrics. In *Thoughts in the Country-Side* (1889), he wrote:

> Here you may walk between the fields and hedges that are as it were one huge nosegay for you, redolent of bean-flowers and clover and sweet hay and elder-blossom. The cottage gardens are bright with flowers...

In his own gardens at Kelmscott, Gloucestershire, and Red House, Bexleyheath, Kent, Morris used informal planting and a mix of herbs and flowers in cottage style.

Morris's declaration that carpet bedding was 'an aberration of the human mind' was used by the garden writer William Robinson (1838–1935) in his 1883 work *The English Flower Garden* and perfectly reflected Robinson's own views. Robinson argued that in the rush for the new exotics and tender plants people had neglected the native plants that suited the English climate and landscape. Writing as editor (and founder) of *Cottage Gardening* in September 1893, Robinson proclaimed that 'among the things made by man nothing is prettier than an English cottage garden'. His vision of a cottage garden was

Opposite: Artists such as Helen Allingham were drawn to the nostalgic image of the country cottage and garden, like this cottage near Brook, Witley, Surrey. Her pictures were in great demand among urban dwellers longing for a simpler way of life.

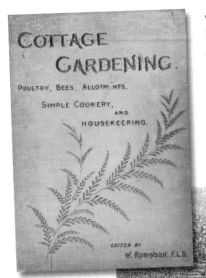

one 'alive with pretty hardy flowers and creepers perfectly suited to their positions – Honeysuckle, Jasmine and old climbing and other Roses', and he noted that these pleasing and artistic gardens were most often found around the cottages of 'poor and simple peoples'. Edged with old tiles or stones, with paths only where necessary, the gardens were full with carnations, lavender, pansies, violas, primroses, aubrietias, dwarf phloxes, border auriculas, larkspur, dahlias, sweet-williams, mignonette and, of course, roses.

William Robinson, champion of the English flower garden, edited the short-lived periodical *Cottage Gardening* during the 1890s.

This Herefordshire cottage garden was etched from one of the photographs sent in to *Cottage Gardening*.

This cottage in Hampshire was described in *Cottage Gardening* as 'simple and picturesque, and with its little patch of vegetables and flowers, it is typical of its class'. The original photograph was sent in by a Mr Mason Good.

Although an essential part of the cottage garden, vegetables were rarely included in paintings and other images. This rare example from *Cottage Gardening* is entitled merely 'A Wayside Garden'.

Robinson ran a photographic competition to capture these joys of the English countryside – and was 'grieved to see among the photographs sent, one of a geometrical arrangement of flowers in rings and patterns entirely the opposite of what a pretty garden should be'. Needless to say, he did not see fit to print it.

Recording country cottages and their gardens for posterity became fashionable as the Industrial Revolution, and later the First World War, made their impact on the social landscape. Gertrude Jekyll, the garden designer and writer, a close friend of William Robinson, recorded the villagers and villages of *Old West Surrey* (1904), illustrated with some of the, more than three hundred, photographs that she took herself. Jekyll believed that it was not the size of a garden that mattered but 'the size of [the owner's] heart and brain' that made a garden delightful or dull. She declared that:

> Some of the most delightful of all gardens are the little strips in front of roadside cottages. They have a simple and tender charm that one may look for in vain in gardens of greater pretension. And the old garden flowers seem to know that there they are seen at their best, for where else can one see such wallflowers, or Double Daisies, or White Rose bushes: such clustering masses of perennial Peas, or such well-kept flowery edges of Pink, or Thrift, or London Pride?

Jekyll was short-sighted and this may have contributed to her keen sense of smell, which led her to prize the old-fashioned primrose, jasmine, violet and mignonette above the double-flowering unscented hybrids. Gorse, birch and bracken had their own sweet smell redolent of the Surrey landscape, and she dismissed the smell of an 'overgrown bed of Pansy plants as rank to offensiveness'. How she felt about pig-sties in the garden she does not record. The old cabbage rose (the Provence rose) was to her the real sweet-smelling rose of the cottage garden.

Not only garden writers enthused over cottage gardens: artists, too, flocked to the countryside to record old thatched cottages and their flower-filled gardens. Among the most famous were Helen Allingham (1848–1926), Myles Birket Foster (1825–99), Henry John King (1855–1924) and Arthur Claude Strachan (1865–1954). Other artists, such as Thomas Hunn (1857–1928), recorded the gardens of middle-ranking country dwellers, including Gertrude Jekyll herself. Helen Allingham (née Paterson) was a friend of Jekyll and knew the same Surrey countryside. After studying at the Government School of Design in Birmingham, the Female School of Art and the Royal Academy Schools, Allingham concentrated on recording Victorian rural life using a technique described as 'entirely opposed to mechanical reproduction … obtaining effects by rubbing, scratching and scrubbing … so that the blooms blend among themselves and grow naturally out of their foliage'. During her forays into the countryside she was often accompanied by Kate Greenaway, the illustrator of children's books. Allingham recorded that they were always made welcome in the gardens or orchards they wished to paint because of the 'scrupulous thoughtfulness for the convenience and

Opposite:
Helen Allingham's painting of the long border at Munstead Wood, the Surrey garden created by Gertrude Jekyll, who much admired cottage garden plants.

feelings of the owners' exhibited by Greenaway. Allingham also painted in
Jekyll's garden at Munstead Wood and produced perhaps the most famous
long border including 'cottage' flowers such as hollyhock, lavender and the
regal lily.

Like paintings and photographs, many early-twentieth-century postcards featured country cottage gardens.

An Old-world country garden.

This rather alarmingly hand-coloured cottage garden bears a romantic message.

SILVER WEDDING DAY GREETINGS.
Just as the moonlight's silver rays
Fall gently o'er the earth,
So may love's radiance light your ways
With joys of truest worth.
T.R 27-8.   H.S.

The most popular of the cottage-garden paintings often included children or animals playing happily in the sunshine. Kittens, hens and ducks gave an added sentimental appeal, along with women in spotless white pinafores carrying equally white laundry (although washing lines were notably absent). Men are rarely shown in these paintings, perhaps because they were away at work when the artists visited, or perhaps they somehow did not fit with the homely image. It has been argued that these images give a false impression of country living, pandering to the tastes of their largely urban purchasers, but comparisons between Allingham's paintings of Surrey and the descriptions and photographs of Jekyll and Robinson suggest that the gardens at least were often as shown.

One of the liveliest of the cottage-garden painters was Theresa Sylvester Stannard (1898–1947), daughter of Henry Sylvester Stannard. Her light, almost animated style was a contrast with the soft romantic quality of earlier female watercolourists. A precocious artist from an artistic background, she exhibited at the Royal Academy in 1915 at the age of sixteen and her work was popular with the Royal Family, who purchased several of her paintings, showing that the cottage garden held appeal even for the most exalted of families.

A winding path, thatched cottage and lilies captured the romantic spirit of the period.

Topiary was a popular feature in Edwardian cottage gardens, seen here in a painting of Old Basing, Hampshire, by Thomas Hunn.

47

RUS IN URBE

Perhaps in response to the restrictions placed on flower gardens in the Second World War, in the 1950s there was a resurgence in the populartiy of the cottage-garden style. It was no wonder that some people, fresh from being enjoined to 'Dig for Victory', with only a 'ribbon of colour' allowed and flower seed supplies restricted, chose to fill their gardens with a flowing floral abundance when peace finally came, although others adhered to annuals in regimented lines. Margery Fish led the way for the cottage-garden movement. In 1937, worried about the possibility of war, Margery and her husband, Walter, bought a cottage and 2-acre plot in East Lambrook, Somerset, commuting between there and London, as many weekend cottagers were to do decades later. The garden was a wilderness, and Margery struggled both with the garden and with her husband, who favoured straight lines and the brightly coloured, regimented style of gardening. By the late 1950s Margery's garden overflowed with plants, in part because of her love of discovering plants that were new to her, and in part through her habit of letting plants self-seed (in her husband's immaculate gravel driveway). Her style was promulgated through her books, in particular *An All the Year Garden* (1958) and *Cottage Garden Flowers* (1961). Margery's favourite flowers were varieties of the traditional cottage garden plants – spikes of mauve *Nepeta* 'Six Hills Giant', the small grey-green leafed *Geranium psilostemon* and the scented *Geranium macrorrhizum*, which will grow in dry places. Primroses were eagerly sought out, and highly prized traditional varieties were planted in the garden and orchard. Penstemons were also among her favourites, and it is fitting that there is now a *Penstemon* 'Margery Fish'.

Vita Sackville-West also popularised the cottage-garden style in the 1950s and 1960s, with the discrete area of garden at Sissinghurst, Kent, fronting on to the small house known as 'The Cottage'. However, the Sissinghurst cottage garden was different from most cottage gardens in that, although the style was abundance, the plants were often the latest hybrids in startling colours of oranges, yellows and reds. The cross-paths in brick and stone harmonised with the architecture of The Cottage, if not with the reds

A rather garish image of an Edwardian cottage garden, owing its abundance to the new 'Plantoids' plant food.

The wartime 'Dig for Victory' campaign had little effect on many cottage gardens, where productivity had always been an essential element, but urban gardeners were encouraged to replace flowers with vegetables.

This selection of cottage-garden seeds dates from the 1950s and shows that the image of the country idyll was alive and well in the post-war austerity years.

and oranges, and originally thyme, pinks and pansies grew in among the cracks in true *laissez-faire* style.

As the suburban population expanded, for most people the phrase 'cottage garden' conjured up either a second home (the 'rural bolthole' of the 1970s) or a countrified adaptation of the long thin urban garden. Anne Scott-James, an author of an earlier history of the cottage garden, was one of those who juggled a weekend rural dream with weekday urban reality. Cross-paths, a vegetable plot, climbing roses, mixed hedging and herbaceous borders were the hallmarks of her garden, which included many of the plants recommended by Margery Fish. Labour-saving is, however, always a constant concern of part-time cottagers, who rarely want to spend the whole weekend tying and staking and watering, and so shrubs often dominate where annuals might once have done, and large areas of lawn carpet the ground where once there would have been productivity and pig-sties.

In the 1980s the cottage-garden style fell out of favour as exotics and hybrids flooded the new garden centres and hard landscaping was the fashion in labour-saving gardens. A whole range of traditional cottage plants, such as the centuries-old pinks, were no longer commercially available. Appropriately, they survived through an informal network of cottage-garden enthusiasts, who in 1982 founded the Cottage Garden Society, open to anyone with an interest in flowers, fruit and vegetables. With the dual aims of encouraging traditional styles of gardening and ensuring that older varieties of plants are not lost, the society arranges garden visits and seed exchanges in a manner reminiscent of the neighbourly gifts of seeds and slips among cottagers through the ages. Soon the cottage garden was being created not just in the country but in the heart of the city. The Cottage Garden Society declared that to create a cottage garden:

> You don't have to live in a cottage, or even in the country! Cottage gardens can be created in the small plots of modern houses, or the narrow gardens of older terraces. The informal style lends itself to any situation.

By 2010 the society had grown to over five-thousand members. This understanding of a cottage garden as a style rather than a location was also one held by Vita Sackville-West. Writing in her column in *The Observer* in the 1950s, she claimed:

> For my own part, if I were suddenly required to leave my own garden and to move into a bungalow on a housing estate, or into a council house, I should have no hesitation at all about ruffling the front garden into a wildly unsymmetrical mess and making it as near as possible into a cottage garden.

Overflowing borders in the garden at East Lambrook Manor, Somerset, created by Margery Fish, who revived the cottage-garden style and saved many traditional plants.

Above: Roses over the walls and cabbages in the garden: the cottage garden and the suburban villa come together.

Descriptions of cottage gardens through the centuries have always emphasised this essential lack of planning and design. In 1892 *Cottage Gardening* declared that 'The charm of the cottage garden is partly due to the absence of any pretentious plan. The walks are what are necessary, and so the little bit of

Right: Surrey cottages such as this one are now often second homes, planted for easy weekend gardening, although the ramblers over the porch remain.

Opposite:
A country cottage garden in the heart of Cambridge: the author's garden and writing studio.

Country comes to town as roses arch welcomingly over a smart door.

ground is there for the flowers to tell their own tale.' Geoff Hamilton, presenter of the BBC television programme *Gardeners' World* from 1979 until 1996, and author of *Geoff Hamilton's Cottage Gardens*, also believed that it was absence of design (alongside the use of traditional techniques and plants) that defined the cottage garden – the gay jostle of herbs, flowers and fruit in unplanned abandon.

Judges at the Royal Horticultural Society's Chelsea Flower Show might beg to differ from this definition, as they have had to appraise numerous cottage-garden entries over the years, each carefully planned and designed. The *Sun* Cottage Garden, designed by Nick Evans and Julie Phipps, won a silver-gilt medal in 2009, and the Thomas Telford Tollhouse Garden, in cottage-garden style, won a silver in 2007. Both were carefully orchestrated to look spontaneous.

In 2010 Channel 4's garden design and planning website recommended that the 'Country Cottage Garden' was ideal for those who 'are looking for a wide range of colour in the garden, [are] keen to grow your own produce and aren't concerned about a formal and organised layout to the garden', while, in his book on designing *Cottage Gardens for Town and Country*, Toby Musgrave allows for various styles, including 'A more formal approach

Every year the Royal Horticultural Society's Chelsea Flower Show exhibits a selection of cottage-style gardens. The Thomas Telford Tollhouse Garden won a silver medal in 2007.

Planting in the Thomas Telford Tollhouse Garden was of native and wild plants combined in the tradition of all cottage gardens.

[which] brings order and symmetry to your garden space with tightly clipped yews and precise planting', and mixes traditional with 'contemporary' planting. Whichever style the modern cottage gardener chooses, the Channel 4 website warns that the cottage-garden style requires 'a keen and enthusiastic gardener with lots of free time to commit' – a reflection on just how far the cottage garden has come since its original inception as a basic larder and medicine chest for the work-weary cottager.

A welcome seat in a country-cottage style garden.

PLANTS FOR THE COTTAGE GARDEN

FLOWERS AND VEGETABLES for the cottage garden have changed little over the centuries; hollyhocks and honeysuckle, sweet-smelling roses and pinks, marigolds and twining convolvulus appear in lists of plants from as early as the sixteenth century. After all, the very essence of the cottage garden is its traditionalism; seeds were carefully hoarded from one year to the next and slips were exchanged with neighbours until all the villagers' gardens were as one. In 1912 M. R. Gloag captured the timeless nature of the English cottage garden and all its flowers:

> A Cottage Garden! Who cannot picture one or more, the memory of which are linked with far off childish days, and the remembrance of the sweet-smelling, gay-coloured, old-fashioned flowers is wafted across the years with a delightful fragrance … Houseleeks and Stonecrops. Flags, Foxgloves, Primroses, Leopard's Bane, clumps of Forget-me-not, mixing their delightful blue with the rich brown of the Wallflowers, all and every kind of flower in turn blossoms gaily'.

However, as hardy plants arrived in Britain from other countries, slowly trickling down the social classes until they reached the humble cottager, new plants began to appear. 'French' marigolds (from South America) joined the traditional calendula, fuchsias dangled their unusual lantern flowers and previously unknown delights of annuals in all colours of the rainbow brightened the pastel borders. Each new arrival was greeted with delight. As Dean Reynolds Hole noted in his book *In Our Gardens* in 1899:

> In the country, the window garden of the cottager is generally filled with geraniums, fuchsias, musk, balsams etc., so highly esteemed that they are often permitted to monopolise the light, and so carefully tended, watered and washed, that their growth and efflorescence are remarkable.

The incomers did not oust the original inhabitants, but took their place among them, so that the Dean also remarked delightedly upon

> the wayside cottages and their bright little gardens ... the Lilacs and Laburnums, the Gilleflowers, the Sweet Williams, and the Cloves, the Bachelor's Button and the Love-lies-bleeding, the Larkspur and the Lupin, the Monthly, the cabbage, the old White Damask, the York and the Lancaster, the Moss and the sweet Briar Rose ... A pretty picture which artists love to paint.

LISTS OF COTTAGE GARDEN PLANTS

Every book on the cottage garden gives a new list of plants, repeating the old but perhaps adding some new or forgotten treasure. Many of the names are redolent of a world of fancy, where children learnt plant names from their parents and had no truck with the Latin nomenclature. As late as 1912 a list of names commonly used for the simple Heartsease pansy included Pretty Pancy, Pink of my John, Love in Idleness, Three Faces under one Hood, Herb Trinity, Cuddle me to you, Pensee and Flame Flower. Many flowers and plants that seem unknown to us when the name is seen in old books can be recognised by reading them out loud. For example, the rather strange looking 'Isop' of the sixteenth and seventeenth centuries becomes our more recognisable 'Hyssop'. What follows is a very small selection of cottage garden plants, with some descriptions taken from the periodical *Cottage Gardening*, 1892–3, and other historic sources.

FLOWERS AND HERBS RECOMMENDED BY WILLIAM LAWSON

The following were recommended by William Lawson in his book *The Country House-wives' Garden* (1618).

FLOWERS FOR THE 'SUMMER GARDEN'

Daffadowndillies	Clove
Hollihock	Gilliflowers
Roses	Pinks
Rosemary	Southernwood
Lavender	Lillies
Bee-Flowres	Sage
Isop	Daisies
Time	Pyony
Cowslips	

HERBS OF MIDDLE GROWTH FOR THE COUNTRY HERB GARDEN

Burrage	Buglosse
Parsly	Sweet Sicily
Flower-deluce	Stock
Gilliflowers	Wall-flowers
Anniseeds	Coriander
Fether-few	Mary-golds
Oculus Christi	Langdibeef
Alexanders	Carduus-benedictus

VICTORIAN COUNTRY COTTAGE GARDEN FLOWERS AND FRUITS

The following plants are among those recommended in *Cottage Gardening* (1892–3) and *The Cottage Garden* (1856).

FLOWERS

Anemone japonica

Aquilegia: 'worthy of a place in every garden, however small'.

Auricula: the original florists' flower.

Canterbury Bells: in cottage shades of blues and pinks

Convolvulus tricolor: 'countryman's trumpets'.

Columbines: named for its resemblance to the Holy Dove, from the Latin *columbaria*.

Cornflowers: brought from the countryside.

Corydalis lutea: called by countryfolk 'wee folk's stockings'.

Daisy: 'The flowers of the daisy appear among the earliest of spring flowers and the colours render a border planted with daisies much more effective than anybody who has not seen it can suppose.'

Delphinium grandiflorum

Eschscholtzia: an introduction from America.

Gaillardia bicolor

Heartsease: also known as Love in Idleness – or love unrequited.

Heliotropes: 'Wherever sweet-scented flowers are admired these highly fragrant and delicately coloured, if not very showy, plants are simply indispensable, while the ease with which they are cultivated brings them within the reach of all.'

Hollyhocks

Hops: 'The hallmark of little Kentish garden plots'.

Larkspur: also known as 'lark's foot'.

Love Lies Bleeding: A strangely exotic plant with its trailing red flowers.

Lychnis: double scarlet of vividest hue; sends up a forest of spikes.

Madonna Lilies: 'Like a procession of beautiful white saints'.

Michaelmas daisies: 'Homely flowers which are fortunately to be found in many cottage gardens … they give charm to the garden which it is not easy to describe.'

Mignonette: 'will be included in everyone's list of sweet smelling plants.'

Old garden tulips: 'The beautiful and richly-coloured Tulips that used to be seen in many cottagers' and farmers' gardens years ago, and which are really descendants of the Florists' Tulips left to their fate in the ordinary garden border or bed, in which they did uncommonly well.'

Peony: 'Nothing could look better against the mellowed stone of the old cottage.'

Perennial sweet pea: 'An effective counter-foil to the dimmed yellow hue of the rose Gloire de Dijon'.

Phlox compacta

Phlox elegantissima

Phloxes: 'There are few flowers that are more admired from July to October than the herbaceous Phloxes.' Phloxes are suited both for small and large gardens.

Pinks: 'The Pink is a most useful flower for small gardens.'

Primroses: 'No cottage garden is complete without Primroses.'

Pulmonaria: called 'the Christmas cowslip' by countryfolk.

Pyrethrum: with their aster-like pure white blooms, and purple and rose in all shades, standing erect.

Rocket

Rosemary: once common in the gardens of the gentry, but by the middle of the eighteenth century said to be found only in the cottage garden.

Some traditional cottage-garden flowers.

Roses: 'A garden without roses is hardly deserving the name of a garden. Lamarque is just the Rose for a warm corner if the house is in favoured southern and western counties. Fortune's Yellow is most beautiful. Gloire de Dijon the best Rose to clothe a Cottage Porch.'

Rue: a bitter herb often grown in the flower beds.

Snapdragons: beloved of children who play with their gentle mouths. The alternative name is Rabbit Mouth or Bunny Mouth.

Solomon's seal: 'One of the most graceful of cottage garden perennials'; the roots a cure for bruises; also called 'David's harp'.

Stocks: 'Colours are so varied and the habit of growth so distinct that one may almost fill a garden with stocks and Chinese Asters.'

Sunflowers

Sweet peas: 'These delightful flowers are not half as well or as widely grown by cottagers as their great merits entitle them to be.'

Sweet-williams: the original cottage garden flower.

Ten-week stocks

Valerian: known for its soothing qualities in tisanes.

Wallflowers: sweet-scented cottage flower.

Yellow fumitory: 'This is a delightful little plant, well known to many of our readers because there is scarcely an old cottage garden in which it may not be found growing on a wall or stony spot.'

Zinnia: these annuals are especially valuable in making the cottager's plot bright.

FRUITS

Apples for against a cottage wall: Ribston Pippin, Brabant Belle Fleur, Lord Nelson, Ganges Pippin, Emperor Alexander.

Eating apples and cooking apples as standards: Winter Red Streak, White Codlin, Irish Codlin, Hoary Morning, Kentish Fillbasket, Tower of Glamis, Blenheim, Lord Suffield, Warner's King, Waltham Abbey Seedling, Echlinville Seedling, Alfriston, Dumelow's Seedling.

Cherries: Black Eagle, May Duke, Elton.

Damsons: Farleigh Prolific.

Gooseberries: 'There is one fruit that can be obtained by the cottager as easily as by the owner of the large garden, and it is a fruit, too, that is fit for any nobleman's table. The Gooseberry is at its best a delicious fruit.' Black Conqueror, British Hero, Red Captain, White Champagne, Green Globe, Red Warrington, Golden Lion, Yellow Champagne, Green Gascoigne, Hedgehog.

Pears: Marie Louise, Jargonelle, Napoleon, Autumn Bergamot, William's Bon Chrétien.

Plums: Green Gage, Orleans, Coe's Golden Drop.

Raspberries: 'It is doubtful whether anything will be found more useful than a patch of raspberries.' Red Antwerp, Yellow Antwerp, Falstaff, Victoria.

Strawberries: Elton Pine, British Queen, Cuthel's Black Prince, Grove-end Scarlet.

VEGETABLES RECOMMENDED FOR COTTAGE CULTIVATION, 1856

Beans: Early Mazagon, Broad Windsor, Dwarf Cluster.

Beans, Kidney or French: Early Dun, Red Speckled.

Beans, Runner: Scarlet Runner, White Runner.

Brussels sprouts: Dwarf Long-Sprouted.

Cabbages: Shilling's Queen, Peacock's Early Dwarf, Dwarf Russian.

Carrots: Early Scarlet Horn, Altringham.

Leeks: Musselburgh, Scotch Flag.

Lettuces: Bath Cos, Brown Dutch.

Onions: Strasburg, White Globe, James's Keeping, Brown Portugal.

Parsnips: Hollow Crowned.

Peas: Prince Albert, Prussian Blue, Woodford's Marrow, Hair's Mammoth, Bishop's Early Long-Podded.

Potatoes: White Round American Early.

Radishes: Early Short Top.

Savoys: Dwarf Green Cape, Marshall's Mammoth.

Turnips: Early Dutch White, Yellow Malta, Robertson's Yellow.

HERBS

Mint, balm, tarragon, chives, marjoram, sage, thyme, sorrel, chervil, hyssop, parsley. In addition, chamomile, fennel, borage, caraway, lavender, rosemary and pennyroyal 'may also find places in the mixed border'.

FURTHER READING

Allingham, Helen, and Stewart, Dick. *The Cottage Homes of England*. Bracken Books, new edition 1991.

Ellacombe, Canon Henry Nicholson. *In a Gloucestershire Garden*. National Trust/Century, reprint 1982.

Fish, Margery. *Cottage Garden Flowers*. Faber & Faber, reprint 1980.

Fish, Margery. *We Made a Garden*. Reprint, Batsford, 2002.

Genders, Roy. *The Cottage Garden*. Pelham Books, 1969.

Jekyll, Gertrude. *The Beauties of a Cottage Garden*. Penguin, 2009.

Lane, Clive. *The Cottage Gardener's Companion*. Cottage Garden Society, 2001.

Lawson, William A. *New Orchard and Garden with the Country House-wives' Garden* (1618). Prospect Books (facsimile), 2003.

Lloyd, Christopher, and Bird, Richard. *The Cottage Garden*. Dorling Kindersley, 1990.

Musgrave, Toby. *Cottage Gardens: Romantic Gardens in Town and Country*. Jacqui Small LLP, 2007.

Philips, Sue. *Cottage Garden Flowers*. RHS Wisley Handbooks, Mitchell Beazley, 2008.

Read, Miss. *The English Vicarage Garden*. Michael Joseph, 1991.

Scott-James, Anne. *The Cottage Garden*. Penguin Books, 1982.

Squire, David. *Victorian Cottage Gardens*. Bramley Books, 1997.

Way, Twigs. *Allotments*. Shire, 2008.

Way, Twigs, *A Nation of Gardeners*. Carlton Press, 2010.

WEBSITES

Plant Heritage: National Council for the Conservation of Plants and Gardens (NCCPG): www.nccpg.com

The Cottage Garden Society: www.thecgs.org.uk

Hardy's Cottage Garden Plants Nursery: www.hardys-plants.co.uk

PLACES TO VISIT

Anne Hathaway's Cottage, Cottage Lane, Shottery, Stratford-upon-Avon,
Warwickshire CV37 9HH. Telephone: 01789 292100.
Website: www.houses.shakespeare.org.uk/anne-hathaways-cottage.html

Hill Top (Beatrix Potter's House), Near Sawrey, Ambleside, Cumbria LA22
0LF. Telephone: 015394 36269. National Trust.

East Lambrook Manor Gardens, East Lambrook, South Petherton, Somerset
TA13 5HH. Telephone: 01460 240328.
Website: www.margeryfish.com

Gilbert White's House and Garden, Selborne, Hampshire GU34 3JH.
Website: www.gilbertwhiteshouse.org.uk

Kelmscott Manor, Kelmscott, Lechlade, Gloucestershire GL7 3HJ.
Telephone: 01367 252486. Website: www.kelmscottmanor.co.uk

Prebendal Manor House and Garden, Nassington, near Peterborough PE8
6QG. Telephone: 01780 782575.
Website: www.prebendal-manor.demon.co.uk

Sissinghurst Castle Garden (including the Cottage Garden), Biddenden Road,
Sissinghurst, near Cranbrook, Kent TN17 2AB.
Telephone: 01580 710701. National Trust.

Smallhythe Place, Smallhythe, Tenterden, Kent TN30 7NG.
Telephone: 01580 762334. National Trust.

Thomas Hardy's Cottage, Higher Bockhampton, near Dorchester, Dorset
DT2 8QJ. Telephone: 01305 262366. National Trust.

Weald and Downland Open Air Museum, Town Lane, Singleton, Chichester,
West Sussex PO18 0EU. Telephone: 01243 811363.
Website: www.wealddown.co.uk

INDEX

Page numbers in italics refer to illustrations

Allingham, Helen *40*, 44, 45, 46
Allotments 17, 32
Arts and Crafts 6, 41
Austen, Jane 28, 29
Bees 15, 26, 36, *39*, 39
Burney, Fanny 27, 28
Carter's Seedsmen 20
Caunton, Nottinghamshire 31
Chelsea Flower Show (RHS) 54
Clare, John 7, 29
Coleworts 9
Cottage Garden Society, The 50–1
Cottage Gardening (periodical) 5, 7, 19, 25, 33, 38, 39, 41, *42*, *43*, 52, 57, 58
Cowper, William 27
Definition (of cottage garden) 5
'Dig for Victory' campaign 48, 49
Dove Cottage, Grasmere *26*, 26, 27
East Lambrook Manor, Somerset 48
Ellacombe, Rev

Henry Thomas and Canon Henry Nicholson 34–5
Fish, Margery 48, 50
Florists' Flowers *16*, 17
Flowers in cottage gardens (lists of) 12, 21, 25, 26, 28, 29, 36, 42, 45, 56–9
Foster, Myles Birket 44
Gooseberries 18, 21, *22*, 22, *23*, 23, 36, 60
Greenaway, Kate 44
Hamilton, Geoff 55
Hardy, Thomas *29*, 29
Hens and 'Poultry' 9, 19, 25, 36, 38–9
Herbs 9, 10, 41, 57, 61
Hogg, Thomas 32
Hole, Samuel Reynolds, Dean of Rochester 31, 32, 38, 56
Hollyhocks 12, 13, 17, 28, 56, 57, 58
Honeysuckle 5, 28, 29, *30*, 31, 41, 42, 56, 57
Horticultural Shows 17–23, 32
Hunn, Thomas *46*
Jasmine 5, 42, 45, Jekyll, Gertrude 14, 44, 45, 46

Ladies of Llangollen (Sarah Ponsonby, Eleanor Butler) 25
Lark Rise to Candleford 35
Lavender 5, *14*, 15, 36, 42, 57
Lawson, William 14, 15
Manure 35, 36
Marigolds *8*, 9, 56
Marrows 5, *21*, 21
Mignonette 5, 42, 45, 58
Morality 5, 19, 31–9
Morris, William *41*
Munstead Wood, Surrey *45*
Olney Vicarage *27*
Paintings of the Cottage Garden 44–7
Paxton, Joseph 35
Pigs 5, 9, 36, *38*, 50
Pinks (Dianthus) 17, 21, 25, 44, 50, 56, 57, 58
Plan, lack of 5, 51, 52, 53
Plas Newydd, Llangollen 25
Rabbits 38, *39*
Robinson, William 38, 41, 43, 44, 46
Roses 5, 7, 15, 25, 26, 41, 44, 52, 56, 57
Sackville-West, Vita 48, 51

Selborne, Hampshire 29
Sense and Sensibility 28
Sissinghurst, Kent 48
Stannard, Theresa 46
Strachan, Arthur Claude 44
The Cottage Gardener (periodical) 31, 38
The Horticultural Magazine 17, 32
Thompson, Flora 35
Tusser, Thomas 12
Uttley, Alison 36
Vegetables and Fruits grown 21, 37, 38, 60–1
Venables, Rev. James 34–5
Vicarage Gardens 34–5
Violets 14, 15
Weald and Downland Open Air Museum, Sussex 10, *11*, 11, 12
Wharram Percy, North Yorkshire 9
White, Rev. Gilbert 29
Wordsworth, William and Dorothy 25, 26, 27